The Amazing World of PLANTS

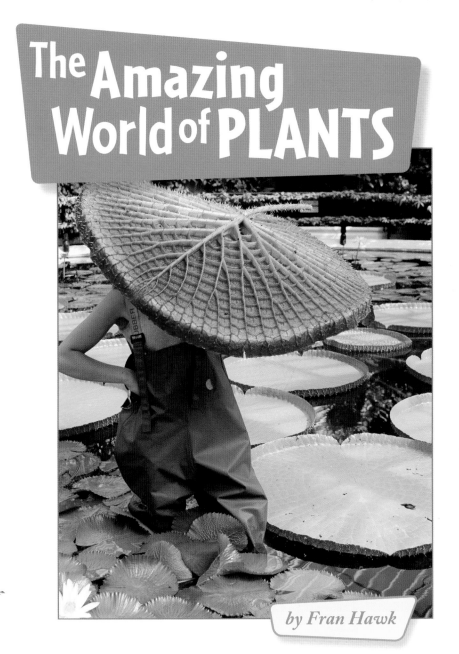

by Fran Hawk

sundance

Program written and developed by Kate Boehm Jerome
in association with Sundance Publishing.

Editorial, Design and Production by Baseline Development Group
in association with Sundance Publishing.

Published by
Sundance Publishing
33 Boston Post Road West
Suite 440
Marlborough, MA 01752
800-343-8204
www.sundancepub.com

Photography:
Cover © Martin Harvey, Gallo Images/CORBIS; p. 1 Jonathan Blair/Getty Images;
p. 3 © Martin Harvey, Gallo Images/CORBIS; pp. 4-5 © Morton Beebe/CORBIS; p. 6
Joel Sartore/Getty Images; p. 7 © LuckyPix/Masterfile; p. 8 Pete Atkinson/Getty Images;
p. 9 © George H. H. Huey/CORBIS; p. 10 (both) David R. Frazier Photolibrary, Inc./Alamy;
p. 11 Edward Parker/Alamy; p. 12 Arnie Rosner/Index Stock Imagery; p. 13 (left) Photo
Resource Hawaii/Alamy, (right) Dorling Kindersley/Getty Images; p. 14 © Royalty-Free/
CORBIS; p. 15 (left) Chel Beeson/Index Stock Imagery, (right) © Michael Boys/CORBIS;
p. 16 (left) © Pixtal/SuperStock, (right) Photographer's Choice/Getty Images; p. 17 (top)
Plantography/Alamy, (bottom) Keren Su/China Span/Alamy; p. 18 (top) Jonathan Blair/Getty
Images, (right) Dave King/DKimages.com, (bottom) Photodisc/Getty Images; p. 19 Photodisc/
Getty Images; p. 20 © David Muench/CORBIS; p. 21 (top) Photodisc/Getty Images, (bottom)
Photodisc/Getty Images; p. 22 © Craig Tuttle/CORBIS; p. 24 © Steve Austin, Papilio/CORBIS;
p. 25 (left) © Dennis Frates/Alamy, (right) © PhotoCuisine/Corbis; p. 26 (top) Martin Harvey/
Getty Images, (bottom) Andrew McRobb/DKimages.com; p. 27 Photodisc/Getty Images;
p. 29 Photodisc/Getty Images

Illustration:
p. 23 Wendy Smith

ISBN: 978-1-4207-0343-6

Printed in China
08/09-225494

Cover photo: Stone plants in bloom

Table of Contents

A Plant Friendly World

Large public gardens offer showy flower and plant displays that draw crowds of people to visit. But gardens don't have to be big to be beautiful. A few pots on a rooftop or balcony can bring great delight, too.

Of course, the pleasing appearance of flowers and plants is not their only important feature. Plants provide oxygen for the air we breathe. Plants feed us. Plants hold soil in place. The list goes on and on.

Life as we know it could not exist without plants. So it's important to take a closer look to learn more about them!

CHAPTER 1

The Nature of Plants

You know animals eat plants. But would you believe there are some plants that eat animals? The sundew plant traps, dissolves, and digests some insects. Digesting bugs is just one of the amazing things that different plants can do!

Got Plants?

As you know, the oxygen we get from plants is essential to our lives. Plants are an important food source, too. Some animals eat plants. Other animals eat the plant-eaters. Think about what you eat yourself. Can you trace a glass of milk all the way back to its plant source?

Even if you haven't thought about it, you've probably eaten just about every part of a plant. This includes the **roots, stems, leaves, fruits, seeds,** flowers, bark, and sap. Hard to believe? Just think about it.

Carrots are roots, and celery is a stem. Lettuce is a leaf, and green peas are seeds. Broccoli is a flower, and cinnamon comes from bark. Maple syrup is made from the sap of the maple tree. There's no doubt about it, plant parts are often a tasty addition to our daily menu.

Pumpkins are fruits that can weigh over 1,000 pounds (about 454 kilograms).

Springing to Life

Plants grow almost everywhere on the planet. They even grow in some places where you might not expect they could live. Plants grow in the shallow, warm waters of the Florida Keys and along the icy shores of Canada's St. Lawrence Seaway. They survive the windy, cold extremes near mountaintops. They also grow in the dusty, hot weather of some deserts.

These plants rely on the sunlight that filters through the shallow water.

The dry Sonoran desert blooms after a spring rain.

In the summer, temperatures in the Sonoran desert in the southwestern United States can climb above 110°F (43°C). The soil is dry because rainfall is scarce. During most months the landscape looks rocky and bare. It's hard to believe that anything could live and grow in such a harsh place.

But you won't believe what happens after a soaking rain finally falls! Seeds that were just waiting for water come to life. The desert that was mostly brown and gray bursts into red, purple, gold, and many other colors. An area that once looked empty is suddenly alive and blooming with colorful plant life.

9

So Many Uses

Plants are very big business—and not just for the farmers who sell plants for food. Some companies use plants to fight pollution. Plants such as alfalfa and clover are used to help clean up soil. Mustard plants can absorb poisonous heavy metals such as lead. Sunflowers work to remove radioactive wastes from water.

Plants also provide raw materials for countless products. Perfumes are made from fragrant flowers. Hats and baskets can be made from plants. Rubber trees are tapped to produce latex, which is used to make erasers and golf balls. Cotton fabric comes from the cotton plant. Baseball bats and paper are made from trees. Wherever we go, whether indoors or outdoors, our lives are enriched by plants.

Sweetgrass is a plant that is used to weave baskets.

Healing Benefits

Long ago, people discovered that some plants contain medicines that help people. Ancient Chinese people used the yarrow plant to ease the pain of a toothache. Cherokee Indians used the goldenseal plant to cure stomachaches. Natives in Peru learned to grind up bark from the cinchona tree to treat the fever of malaria.

Chemicals from plants are still a part of many useful medicines today! Willow bark can be used to reduce pain and fever. A chemical from periwinkle plants is used in a medicine that treats leukemia. Every day scientists all over the world search for new ways to use chemicals from plants to treat or cure diseases. That's one of the reasons why it's so important to protect the places where different plants live.

BLUE PLANET Note

The rosy periwinkle plant is native to the rainforests of Madagascar. Healers on this island first used rosy periwinkle to treat diabetes. This led scientists to study the plant and discover its cancer-fighting benefits.

Rosy periwinkle

CHAPTER 2

Basic Plant Parts

Plants cannot run from their enemies or move to find fresh sources of water. So how do they stay alive? Plants depend on their different parts to help them get the things they need.

The Parts That Make the Whole

Most plants have three basic parts—roots, stems, and leaves. But these parts can have many different looks. For example, the leaves of a taro plant can grow to be three feet (almost a meter) wide. The stem of a prickly pear cactus is thick and dotted with tiny spines.

Even though roots, stems, and leaves may look different from plant to plant, they all have basic functions. These functions keep the plant alive.

Tiny red fruits dot this cactus (right). Taro plants, also called elephant ear, are grown for food in Hawaii (below).

13

Anchor in Place

If you start at the bottom of a plant, you can quickly get to the root of the matter! Some plants, like grasses, have roots that spread out over large areas near the surface of the ground. Other plants have roots that go deep down into the soil. The water lily's roots dangle far below the surface of the water. They anchor the plant in the muddy bottom of a pond.

The anchoring job of roots is key. Without roots to hold them in place, a stiff wind or a heavy rain could easily knock plants over. But plants continue to stand their ground even in bad weather because roots are holding them in place.

As they anchor a plant, roots also help keep the soil around a plant in place. In fact, one of the best ways to keep soil from eroding, or blowing or washing away, is to put plants in the dirt to hold it in place.

Tulips grow from bulbs and have hairlike roots that anchor them in place.

The roots of this mangrove tree (above) help prop it up in water. This parsnip (right) is actually a taproot.

Absorb and Store

Roots do more than just hold plants and soil in place. They also absorb, or take things in, from the soil. Roots absorb water. They also absorb minerals. These essential ingredients are needed for the plant to make its own food and grow.

If a plant has a **taproot** system, it has one main root that is thicker than the others. A taproot can store food for a plant. When you munch on a carrot, you are actually eating a taproot. The food that was originally stored for the plant is now serving as food for you.

Standing Tall

Like roots, stems also come in many shapes and sizes. Strawberry stems, called runners, look like soft, delicate threads running along the ground. But the trunk, or stem, of a large redwood tree can be wide enough to drive a car through. The stems of large trees and shrubs are **woody stems.** This means they grow much thicker to support the bigger plants.

It's not hard to guess the main job of stems when you're looking at a tall redwood tree! A stem supports a plant. This helps the other parts of the plant, such as the branches, flowers, and leaves, do their jobs. For example, a strong stem holds leaves up to face the sky. This allows the leaves to get the sunlight they need to make food.

A redwood tree (above) can grow as tall as a 25-story building. A sunflower (right) can reach 10 feet tall.

Bamboo is a woody plant that can grow as much as 3 feet (about 1 meter) per day.

A stem's second task is to serve as a plant's transportation system. Tubelike structures act like tiny straws inside the stem to move material around the plant. Small tubes called **xylem** (ZI-lem) carry minerals up from the roots to the leaves of the plant. Other tubes, called **phloem** (FLO-em), move food from the leaves to all of the other parts of the plant.

17

The largest water lilies in the world (above) can grow up to 6 feet (2 meters) wide. Necklace plants (right) have an unusual shape.

Living Factories

When you hear the word *leaves* you might immediately picture the broad, green leaves of many trees. But the leaves of some plants can look very different from this. The raffia palm can grow leaves over 80 feet (about 24 meters) long. The leaves of a necklace plant look as if they have been threaded on a string.

No matter what their size, the leaves of most plants are used for one thing—to make food. Plants are like living factories. They use processes to make products. **Chlorophyll,** the chemical that gives many leaves their green color, traps energy from sunlight. Then **photosynthesis,** the food-making process, can begin.

The Food-Making Machine

Photosynthesis is important in two ways. First, it helps make food for plants. Second, it provides oxygen for the air, which is what we breathe to live.

There are two main steps in the process of photosynthesis. In the first step, light energy trapped by the chlorophyll is used to split water into oxygen and hydrogen. The oxygen becomes part of the air. In the second step, hydrogen combines with carbon dioxide to make sugar. This sugar is stored as food for the plant.

So how does a plant use its stored food? Plants can use oxygen to break apart the sugars they have already stored. This process, called **respiration,** releases energy for the plant to use at any time of the day or night.

Photosynthesis is an important plant process.

Light energy is trapped

Oxygen is released

Sugars

Carbon dioxide is taken in

Water comes up from roots

CHAPTER 3

Grow, Plants, Grow!

The Great Basin National Park is home to some of the oldest living trees in the world. This bristlecone pine grows very slowly and can live for more than 4,000 years! How can a small seed survive in this harsh environment to become a full-grown tree? It's a very special process.

To Seed or Not to Seed

Scientists divide plants into two groups according to whether or not they grow from seeds. Pine trees, such as the bristlecone pine, grow from seeds—but not all plants do. A few plants, such as mosses and ferns, grow from structures called spores.

Most of the plants you see every day are seed plants. A big group of seed plants includes the **conifers.** Pine, fir, spruce, and redwood trees are conifers. They grow cones that contain seeds of many shapes and sizes. Most conifers are also called evergreens. These trees don't lose their leaves in the winter. They stay "ever-green" all year.

Another group of seed plants includes all of the **flowering plants.** Roses, lilacs, and other flowering plants don't have cones. They need flowers to make seeds.

Both conifers (like these pine cones) and flowering plants (like this bird of paradise) are seed plants.

Parts of a Flowering Plant

Flowers are perhaps the most beautiful part of a plant. But decoration is not their main purpose. Flowers are needed to make seeds—and most flowering plants have four main parts to help do this: **sepals, petals,** a **pistil,** and **stamens.**

The sepals (SEE-puls) are green leaflike parts that protect the bud before it blooms. As the bud grows bigger and gets ready to open, the sepals are forced farther and farther apart.

When the bud bursts into bloom, we see and smell the scent, color, and shape of the petals. The petals attract butterflies, birds, bees, and other animals that are needed in the seed-making process.

Mountain meadows are filled with different types of wildflowers.

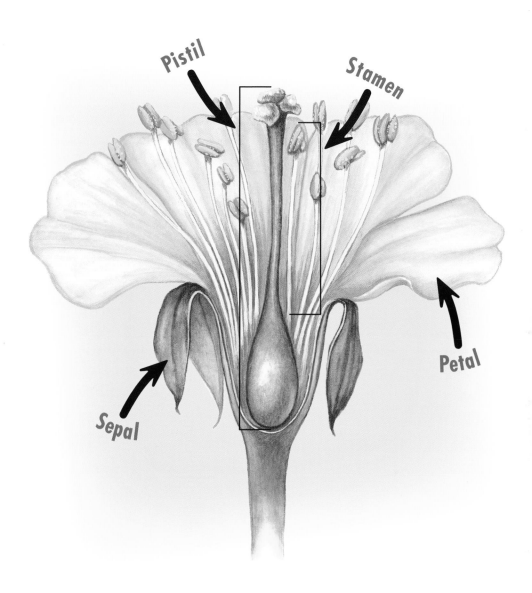

Pistil

Stamen

Petal

Sepal

The pistil is found right in the center of the ring of petals. It makes the eggs that the flower needs to make seeds. But the eggs cannot develop into seeds until they combine with the sperm that's produced by **pollen.**

So what part of the plant makes the pollen? It happens in the stamens. Stamens surround the pistil in the center of the flower.

Pollen on the Move

Moving pollen from the stamens (where it's made) to the pistil (where it needs to be) is called **pollination.** Sometimes a plant can get its own pollen to its own pistil. But most often, pollen has to be moved from one plant to another.

How does that happen? Plants have some pretty interesting ways to get their pollen shuttled around. In many cases, insects are involved. Brightly colored petals attract bees to a flower. While the bee is in the center of the flower collecting food, pollen gets stuck on its legs and back. When the bee lands on the next flower looking for more food, the pollen on its legs may rub off on the stamen of that flower. Presto! The pollen is exactly where it needs to be.

Bats, birds, and tiny animals also participate in pollination. In addition, wind carries pollen from plant to plant. If you're allergic to pollen, you may get watery eyes and start sneezing when wind is blowing pollen through the air.

Seeds mature at different rates. Fruits protect them as they develop.

Seed Time

When the sperm from the pollen meets the egg in the pistil, **fertilization** occurs. This means a seed can now develop.

Since most of the parts of a flower are no longer needed after fertilization, they die and fall away. But the part that contains the egg cells slowly begins to grow into a fruit. From watermelons to grapes, fruits come in many different sizes. But they all serve the same function. The fruit protects the seeds while they grow. When fruits are ripe, it means that their seeds are ready to grow into new plants.

This coconut that has washed up on shore has begun to sprout a new tree.

Getting Around

Seeds can't walk or run, but they certainly get around! Coconuts float great distances and wash up on beaches to grow in a new place. Burrs, which are hard, prickly fruits with seeds inside, stick to an animal's fur for a free ride to a new place in the neighborhood.

When a ripe kiwi falls off a tree and rots on the ground, some of the seeds inside may grow into a new kiwi tree. And after birds and animals eat ripe fruits, they deposit seeds in their droppings. Some plants have seedpods that burst and scatter the seeds into the air, where the wind may carry them for miles. Squirrels eat some of the acorns they gather and bury the rest. A forgotten acorn can grow into an oak tree.

BLUE PLANET Note

An engineer named George de Mestral studied the hooks and loops that make burrs stick. He invented Velcro™ by imitating the same hooks and loops!

26

Protecting Plants

The more we know about plants, the better we are able to protect and use them. It takes an international effort to preserve rainforests around the world. And it takes many scientists years of study to identify medicines in plants that could help cure diseases.

But the local "keep off the grass" signs are just as important! Preserving green spaces in the neighborhoods around us helps to improve the environment in many ways. For example, parks with trees and grass growing in the middle of a city can help lower high summer temperatures. Having plenty of green plants around also improves the quality of the air we breathe.

Earth is a "plant planet." Life here would not exist as we know it without the plants you see all around you. What will the future bring to our planet? No one knows for sure. But chances are, the greener we stay, the better off we'll be!

Helping out in a community garden can improve the environment and the neighborhood.

Tuesday: Writing Assignment

Planting for the Future

Your school recently bought several acres of empty land. The school board is asking students to come up with proposals for how to use it.

Some people want to use it as a parking lot. Others think it would make a great soccer field. But you think it would be a good spot for a community garden.

As you write your proposal, consider what you now know about plants. First, you'll need to convince the board that plants are important. Then, you'll need to convince them that you understand plants, so they'll know the project is in good hands.

posted by BluePlanetXpert / 3:45 PM / Comments 0

Instant Message

Subject:
The Root of Life

>**flowerpwr:** How do plants support the environment?

BluePlanetXpert: One important way is through their foodmaking process, photosynthesis. Plants take in carbon dioxide and release oxygen, which we need to breathe.

>**flowerpwr:** So you could say plants help improve the quality of life?

BluePlanetXpert: Yes, in many ways, such as providing food and shade.

Blue Planet Chat Room

Subject:
Growin' Good Things

>**flowerpwr:** What plants should I propose?

sprout07: I think it depends on what the soil is like.

carrotTOP: Yeah, and how shady it is. I think we should plant some vegetables, though.

bugsy: Me, too. And we'll need a fence to keep the deer out.

Glossary

chlorophyll green substance in leaves that traps energy from sunlight for use in photosynthesis

conifers seed plants that produce seeds in cones

fertilization the plant process in which sperm combine with eggs to make seeds

flowering plants seed plants that produce flowers and fruits that contain seeds

fruits structures formed by flowering plants that contain the seed or seeds

leaves the parts of a plant where photosynthesis usually takes place

petals the usually colorful parts of a flower that surround the pistil and stamens

phloem tubelike structures in a plant's stem that transport food from the leaves to all of the other parts of the plant

photosynthesis the process that takes place in green plants in which energy from sunlight is used to make food

pistil the part of a flower where egg cells are produced

pollen tiny grains that contain sperm that will join with eggs to form seeds

pollination the process that moves pollen from the stamens to the pistil of a flower

respiration the process that uses oxygen to release energy and gives off carbon dioxide

roots the plant parts that support the plant, gather nutrients from the soil, and sometimes store food

seeds the parts of a plant that can germinate to grow a new plant

sepals the leaflike coverings that protect the buds of flowering plants

stamens the parts of flowers that make pollen

stems the parts of plants that support the leaves and carry water and food

taproot a thick, main root that grows deep into the ground

woody stems the thick, stiff stems that support trees and shrubs

xylem tubelike structures in a plant's stem that carry water and minerals from the roots to the leaves

Index